NATURE FILES

ANIMAL MOVEMENT

NATURE FILES – ANIMAL MOVEMENT
was produced by

David West 👥 **Children's Books**
7 Princeton Court
55 Felsham Road
London SW15 1AZ

Designer: Julie Joubinaux
Editor: Gail Bushnell
Picture Research: Carlotta Cooper

First published in Great Britain by Heinemann Library, Halley Court, Jordan Hill, Oxford OX2 8EJ, part of Harcourt Education. Heinemann is a registered trademark of Harcourt Education Ltd.

07 06 05 04 03
10 9 8 7 6 5 4 3 2 1

ISBN 0 431 18244 2 (HB)
ISBN 0 431 18251 5 (PB)

British Library Cataloguing in Publication Data

Petty, Kate
Animal movement. - (Nature files)
1. Animal locomotion - Juvenile literature
I. Title
591.4'79

Printed and bound in Italy

PHOTO CREDITS :
Abbreviations: t-top, m-middle, b-bottom, r-right, l-left, c-centre.

Front cover - tr (Jeff Foott), mr & l (Hans Christoph Kappel) naturepl.com, b - (Manoj Shah) Getty Images. Pages 3 & 23b (Doug Allan), 5t, 10br, 11bm, 27l (Peter Oxford), 5b, 16b (John Cancalosi), 6t & 17bl (Hanne & Jens Eriksen), 8 (Tony Heald), 9t (Karl Ammann), 10t (Nick Gordon), 11bl (Lynn M. Stone), 11br (Flip de Nooyer), 12–13b (Staffan Widstrand), 14–15, 24b, 25tl (Jeff Foott), 15b (Premaphotos), 16t (Jim Clare), 17t, 18t (Dietmar Nill), 17r, 28–29t (Thomas D. Mangelsen), 18b, 19bl, 27r (Hans Christoph Kappel), 21t (Avi Klapfer Rotman), 21b (Fabio Liverani), 22br (Sue Daly), 23l (Jeff Rotman), 24t, 29r (Jurgen Freund), 25b (Richard du Toit), 26t (Tom Vezo), 26b (Warwick Sloss), 28 (Tom Walmsley) - naturepl.com. 4t (Ted Schiffman), 7l (Matt Meadows), 9m (Norbert Wu), 10l (Burton - UNEP), 19t (Alain Compost) - Still Pictures. 4b, 20 both - Corbis Images. 6m (Tim Hellier), 7r (Roger Steene), 13l, 14t, 22l (Peter Parks), 21m (Masa Ushioda), 22t (James D. Watt) - Image Quest 3D. 6–7 - The Culture Archive. 9b (Stan Osolinski), 11t (Brian Kenney), 12–13t (Satoshi Kuribayashi), 15t (Harold Taylor), 19br (Richard Packwood), 28–29b (Howard Hill), 29l (Max Gibbs), 13r - Oxford Scientific Films. 25tr - Michael & Patricia Fogden.

Every effort has been made to contact copyright holders of any material reproduced in this book. Any omissions will be rectified in subsequent printings if notice is given to the publishers.

An explanation of difficult words can be found in the glossary on page 31.

NATURE FILES

ANIMAL MOVEMENT

Kate Petty

Heinemann
LIBRARY

CONTENTS

Soaring thousands of metres above the ground, birds make flying look easy. Their secret is broad, aerodynamic wings to maximise lift, and light, hollow bones to minimise drag.

Powerful tail muscles propel a fish through the water. Although water is 800 times denser than air, some fish can move almost as quickly as the fastest land animal.

INTRODUCTION

The ability to move is one of the things that sets animals apart from the rest of the living world. From a termite that burrows through solid wood to an eagle that soars over mountains, from the breathtaking sprint of a cheetah to the lumbering plod of a tortoise, the ways in which animals move are as diverse and as fascinating as animals themselves.

A centipede's long, flexible body and many legs allow it to scuttle quickly across the forest floor where it makes its home.

With its muscular hind limbs, a kangaroo can leap 6 metres in a single bound. Its long tail is used for balance, but it also makes it impossible for the kangaroo to move backwards.

Whether they run, fly, swim, slither or burrow, almost all animals use muscles and skeletons to drive their movements.

MUSCLES

Most animals move by using muscles, bundles of tissue that can contract and relax. Muscles are usually grouped together in pairs – one contracts while the other relaxes for movement in one direction, then the first relaxes while the second contracts to move back in the other direction.

Birds that are capable of flight have powerful chest muscles to produce the downwards motion of the wings that lifts them off the ground.

This sequence of photos shows a horse moving. The places where its legs bend are the joints between different bones, and the outlines of the powerful muscles are visible through its skin.

Many flying insects can contract and relax their wing muscles hundreds of times a second to achieve rapid flight.

SKELETONS

To provide movement, muscles need to be attached to something solid. In vertebrates (animals with backbones) this is an internal skeleton made of bone or cartilage. Some invertebrates, such as insects, have a rigid external skeleton. Others, such as worms, have an internal, fluid-filled skeleton.

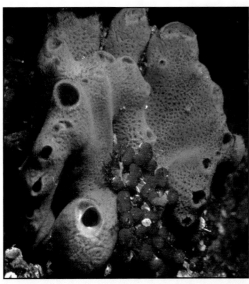

Amazing FACT

Sponges are some of the simplest of all animals, and also the least mobile. Adult sponges spend their entire lives in one place. But their larvae, which grow on the adults like buds, roam the sea, until they eventually find a rock to attach themselves to.

Sponges filter food from the sea.

A snake has chains of muscle running the length of its body. These are attached to its spine and ribs, giving it great flexibility.

For land animals, running is the best way to get somewhere fast. Long legs and good balance are vital to both predators and prey.

TWO LEGS OR FOUR?

Humans and birds run on two legs, but the fastest land animals all run on four. This gives them twice as much pushing power, as well as better balance. Big feet can slow you down, so fast cats run on the tips of their toes. Horses and antelopes have hard hooves so that they can run long distances.

With its strong legs and flexible knees, an ostrich can achieve speeds of 70 kilometres per hour – as fast as a racehorse.

COILED SPRINGS

The cheetah is the fastest animal on four legs. It can reach speeds of more than 100 kilometres per hour, because its body is designed like a spring. As it runs, it brings its hind legs in front of its fore legs, and its long, flexible backbone arches up like a coiled spring. When the backbone arches down, the energy stored in the spring is released. This pushes the cheetah forwards at great speed.

Coiled

Backbone arches up.

A cheetah at full stretch.

Uncoiled

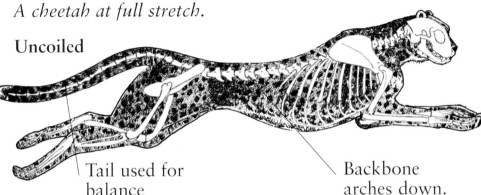

Tail used for balance

Backbone arches down.

HUNTERS AND HUNTED

In terms of top speeds, predators usually have the advantage over their prey. A cheetah can hit 115 kilometres per hour, and a lion can run almost as fast as a racehorse. But they can only reach these speeds in very short bursts. The animals they are chasing may not be as fast, but they will always have the edge over longer distances.

If they don't get caught in the first few seconds of the chase, pronghorn antelopes have a good chance of escaping from a pursuing predator.

Amazing FACT

The basilisk lizard can do the seemingly impossible – walk on water! The lizard can run very fast on two legs. It is also very light and has wide, flat feet, so it can run long distances across water. But it has to keep its speed up – if it slows down, it will sink.

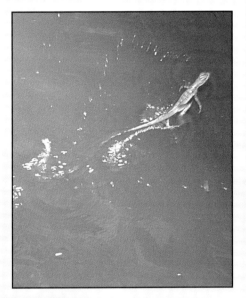

Basilisks run if threatened.

9

Many animals are well suited to climbing, either on mountains or in trees. Living high up gives them protection from predators, and access to plentiful sources of food.

MOUNTAIN HOMES

Mountain peaks that humans find almost impossible are home to many amazingly sure-footed animals. Yaks may look clumsy, but they can pick their way across Himalayan slopes at 6000 metres above sea level. Mountain goats have large hooves with tough outer rims for protection and soft inner pads to grip on to slippery surfaces.

The squirrel monkey has a prehensile tail – it can grip like a hand. It's like having a fifth limb, which is useful for moving among the treetops.

Mountain goats (left) are comfortable even on steep rock faces. The day gecko (below) has feet covered in hairs, called setae, which are tipped with suction pads. These pads allow the gecko to cling to vertical surfaces.

SWINGING GIBBON

Although gibbons can walk on two legs, 90% of their movement is by brachiation – using the arms to swing from place to place. Their long arms and hooked fingers allow them to grasp branches easily. Gibbons are extremely agile in the treetops, and can leap gaps of 10 metres or more, although they never cross water, as they cannot swim.

LIFE IN THE TREES

Animals that live in trees need hands, feet or claws that can grip tree trunks and branches. Tree-dwelling monkeys have long fingers on their hands and feet. Some birds and lizards have feet like pincers for gripping branches. Squirrels can run up and down tree trunks using their sharp claws.

Gibbons have longer arms than legs.

North American porcupines are excellent climbers who spend much of their lives in trees. They have long claws and rough footpads for extra grip.

Amazing FACT

If a hoatzin chick falls out of its nest, it can climb back up again using a claw on each wing. Chicks lose their claws as they grow, but adult hoatzins still use their wings to clamber around in the branches.

Claw on a hoatzin chick's wing.

HOPPING AND JUMPING

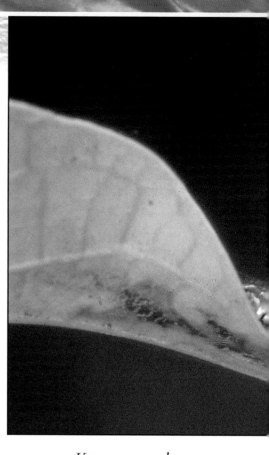

Hopping and jumping are fast ways of moving. They are also efficient in terms of how much energy they use. Animals that are designed for hopping usually have long, extremely powerful hind legs.

HOPPING MAD

Rabbits, kangaroos and frogs move by hopping. They all have hind legs that are at least twice as long as their front legs, and their lower legs and ankles are especially elongated, or stretched out. Hopping can be a speedy way to travel – red kangaroos can reach speeds of 60 kilometres per hour.

Kangaroos have elastic tendons in their legs. On landing, these tendons are stretched like rubber bands, storing up energy for the next jump.

HOW A FROG LEAPS

A frog leaps with three simultaneous movements: its front legs arch to make the body face upwards; its feet push off from the ground; and its hind legs straighten quickly, launching it into the air. It lands with its front legs stretched out to absorb the impact, and its hind legs already set for another leap.

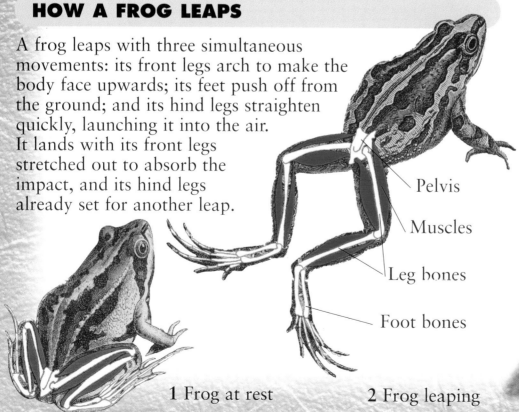

Pelvis

Muscles

Leg bones

Foot bones

1 Frog at rest   2 Frog leaping

INSECT JUMPERS

Grasshoppers and fleas are top insect jumpers. To escape from predators, grasshoppers leap high into the air, then spread their wings and fly. Fleas' legs contain an elastic substance called resilin which stores energy like a bow. When the energy is released suddenly, the flea is fired into the air.

Jumping spiders use their four back legs for pouncing on their prey. With their excellent eyesight they are masters at judging the distance they have to jump.

Amazing FACT

Relative to its size, the flea is the greatest jumper of them all. It can jump 25 centimetres in the air, which is over 150 times its own height. An adult human who could jump the equivalent height would be able to clear St. Paul's Cathedral in a single bound!

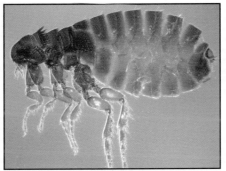

A dog flea.

If it gets stuck on its back, a click beetle can flip itself the right way up. It flexes its body, then snaps it back again violently, launching itself into the air.

13

CREEPING AND CRAWLING

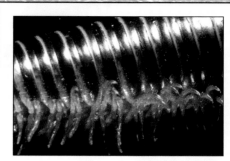

Millipede showing legs.

How do you get around if you have no legs – or hundreds of them? Worms, snakes, millipedes and other creepy-crawlies all have their own methods.

CRAWLING

Earthworms crawl through soil by contracting some parts of their bodies while expanding others. Some snakes also move like this when underground or stalking prey.

A snake moves by throwing its entire body into curves and pushing against rough surfaces with the sections on the inside of the curves to move it forwards.

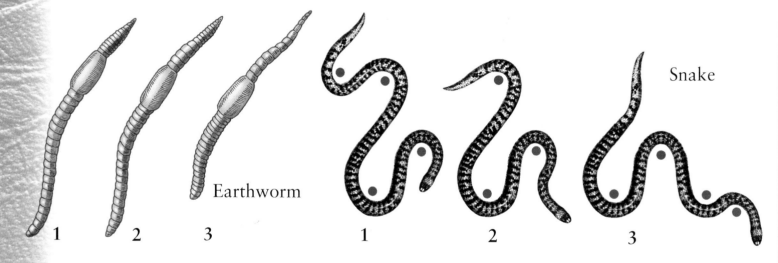

Earthworm

1   2   3

Snake

1   2   3

SLITHERING AND SLIDING

The way that snakes and worms move is called axial movement – they use their whole bodies for movement rather than body parts like legs, wings or flippers. Worms burrow through the earth by squeezing into a small space, and then expanding their soft bodies to create a tunnel. Because of their bony skeletons, snakes are not as flexible as worms, but their shape enables them to move easily through narrow spaces.

Amazing FACT

Although the name 'millipede' means '1000 feet', none actually have that many. Most have between 100 and 300 legs, although one species from California has 750! Millipedes' legs move in waves as they walk.

SIX-LEGGED WALKERS

All insects have six legs. When they walk they first move their front right leg, middle left leg and back right leg, then their front left leg, middle right leg and back left leg. This way they always keep three legs on the ground at any one time, making them very stable. Some insects can move very fast this way – a tiger beetle from Australia can cover 171 times its own body length per second!

Looper caterpillars move by arching their bodies to move their back legs forwards, then stretching out their front legs.

Sidewinder snakes move across the sand by supporting their weight on two or three points and throwing the rest of their body forwards in loops.

Despite their small size, a swarm of ants on the move can be a formidable sight. A swarm can consist of tens of thousands of insects, and it can do considerable damage to anything in its way.

15

Birds are the undisputed masters of flight. With their feathered, streamlined bodies, light bones and aerodynamic wings they are perfectly adapted for life in the air.

IN A FLAP

All birds flap their wings to get airborne. With their powerful chest muscles, they push downwards to lift themselves into the air. On the upstroke, the wings are twisted so that they cut through the air, and the cycle begins again.

Hummingbirds can hover in one place, allowing them to feast on nectar with their long beaks. They beat their wings in a figure-of-eight pattern up to 80 times a second.

WINGS

Like the wing of an aeroplane, a bird's wing is shaped to provide lift, the force that keeps it airborne. Because the wing is angled, air passing under the wing is forced downwards. Air passing over the wing 'sticks' to the upper surface, and is also angled downwards. This downwards movement of air pushes the bird up.

Air moving over wing

Lift

Wing shape

Air moving under wing

A swan runs across water to take off.

Soft downy feathers on an owl's wings allow it to fly almost silently. Its prey won't know the owl is swooping down on it until it's too late.

SOARING HIGH

Flapping uses up lots of energy, so once they are in the air, many large birds stay there by soaring. As air heats up, it rises, creating an updraft. Birds fly into an updraft and 'ride' it upwards, without having to flap their wings. At the top of the updraft they glide gently downwards until they reach the next one.

Amazing FACT

The peregrine falcon is easily the fastest animal in the world. It roams the sky searching for its prey – smaller birds. In level flight it is almost as fast as a cheetah. But when it spots its prey it goes into a near-vertical dive, reaching an amazing 360 kilometres per hour. It kills its prey on impact.

Peregrine falcon.

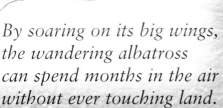

By soaring on its big wings, the wandering albatross can spend months in the air without ever touching land.

17

Apart from birds, only bats and some insects are true fliers. However, some mammals and reptiles are able to glide through the air.

The bones in a bat's wing are similar to the bones in a human's hand. Their extra-long finger bones form a frame, with a thin web of skin stretched tight between them.

FURRY FLIERS

Although bats and birds are not closely related, they share many characteristics that make them effective fliers. They both have lightweight bone structures, strong chest muscles, and front limbs which have been modified into wings. But bats are covered with fur, not feathers.

INSECT FLYERS

In insects with fast wingbeats, the wings are not directly attached to the flight muscles. Instead a group of muscles links the top and bottom of the body. When these muscles contract, the top of the body is pulled down and the wings, which are hinged, move upwards. When the muscles relax, the wings snap down again.

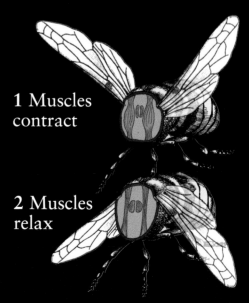

1 Muscles contract

2 Muscles relax

With its rapid wingbeat, the hawk-moth can fly at 53 kilometres per hour. The humming-bird hawk-moth can fly backwards by reversing its wingbeat pattern.

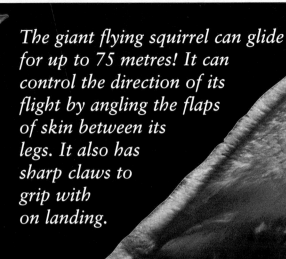

The giant flying squirrel can glide for up to 75 metres! It can control the direction of its flight by angling the flaps of skin between its legs. It also has sharp claws to grip with on landing.

GRACEFUL GLIDERS

Animals that glide cannot fly upwards, but they travel long distances by slowing their fall like a parachutist. Gliding mammals usually have a flap of skin called a patagium which hangs between the front and hind legs. When they leap into the air they spread their legs to stretch out the patagium. In flying lizards, extended ribs support a similar flap of skin.

Amazing FACT

A type of midge from the *forcipomyia* group of midges can beat its wings 62,760 times per minute. It takes 0.00045 seconds for its wing muscles to contract and relax – the fastest muscle movement of any animal.

Swarms of midges above a river.

The front wings of beetles are modified to form a hard casing for their thin hind wings. The casing has to be opened and held out during flight.

19

SUPER SWIMMERS

Land animals push off from solid surfaces to set themselves in motion. Sea creatures have to push against the water to thrust their bodies along. Fish, penguins, seals and even octopuses all have streamlined shapes for cutting smoothly through water.

Amazing FACT

With its ultra-streamlined shape and unusual fin, the sailfish is officially the fastest fish in the sea, clocking in at an amazing 109 kilometres per hour! That's fast enough to leave most speedboats behind, although the sailfish can only keep up such high speeds for short periods of time.

HOW A FISH SWIMS

Fish swim with their tails. Powerful muscles wave the tail from side to side, pushing against the water and propelling the fish forwards. The tail fin can add extra power.

The dorsal fins (on its back) and the pectoral fins (at the sides) help the fish to keep upright and act as rudders to steer the fish's body.

Sharks are powerful swimmers, able to reach high speeds, turn quickly, and in some cases leap out of the water. These abilities make them highly effective ocean predators.

Many small fish swim together in large groups called shoals. Quick reflexes and agile bodies help all the fish to turn and change direction at the same time.

Pacific sailfish cruising in Costa Rica.

STAYING AFLOAT

Most fish have a swim bladder like a small balloon that fills up with gas when the fish wants to stay high up in the water, and empties when it wants to go lower. Sharks do not have swim bladders and start to sink if they stop swimming. Their pectoral fins are fairly rigid, so they cannot 'put the brakes on' as other fish can.

Like fish, these dolphins use their tails to swim, but they move them up and down rather than from side to side, so that the flattened tail fin can push against the water. The spines of all mammals are more flexible this way. Try touching your toes by bending forwards, and then try it sideways!

FISH OR MAMMAL?

Whales and dolphins are mammals, so they are more closely related to humans and horses than to fish. But a life in the water has made them adapt until their body shapes are very similar to those of fish. The hind legs found in land mammals have disappeared, and the front legs have evolved into flippers like a fish's fins.

The mudskipper is an incredible fish that uses its fins to 'walk' on land. Some species can even climb trees!

21

Fish are not the only animals to move through the water with ease. Other sea creatures use different ways of getting around, from aimless drifting to jet propulsion.

GOING WITH THE FLOW

Some sea creatures rely on winds and ocean currents to carry them from one place to another. One of these is the Portuguese man-of-war, which is in fact a whole colony of jellyfish-like polyps attached to a gas-filled swim bladder. Small fish and crustaceans get trapped in its poisonous, 20-metre-long tentacles.

Nautiluses can reach 20 cm across.

Amazing FACT

The nautilus, a mollusc that lives in the South Pacific, has gas-filled buoyancy chambers to stop it sinking. As the animal grows, extra chambers are added to its spiral-shaped shell. A tube running through these chambers releases gas to keep it floating in an upright position.

The Portuguese man-of-war can deflate its swim bladder in rough water to protect it from damage.

A starfish's arms are covered in tiny tube feet. The feet are tipped with suction pads that pull the starfish along.

JET PROPULSION

A squid moves by jet propulsion that works a bit like the jet engines on an aeroplane. First it sucks water into the mantle (a fold of flesh around its body). Then it squirts a high-pressure jet of water out of its funnel, propelling it in the opposite direction.

High-pressure water jet

Muscles squeeze cavity.

Water sucked into mantle

Direction of travel

When startled, a giant octopus can jet away from danger quickly.

ROCK BOTTOM

Instead of floating, many animals that live in water move along the sea bottom. Animals with legs, like crabs and lobsters, scuttle along the sea-floor just as they do on land. They can move slightly faster in water, because the buoyancy increases their stability. Starfish and sea urchins slowly drag themselves along using rows of tiny suckers. Leeches creep across the sea-floor with suckers at each end of their soft bodies.

Although clumsy on land, the penguin's streamlined body and agile movements make it a successful underwater hunter.

Animals that can barely move themselves can still travel – by hitching a lift! Some travelling companions are more welcome than others.

A HOME FOR LIFE

Some sea creatures, like limpets, coral polyps and sea anemones, stay in one place all the time, using their feathery limbs or tentacles to flick food towards them. Barnacles usually cling to rocks, but if they hitch lifts with sea turtles or whales they can travel great distances without moving.

When sea anemones stick to the shell of a hermit crab, they both benefit. The sea anemones get food and transport, while they protect the crab from enemies with their stinging tentacles.

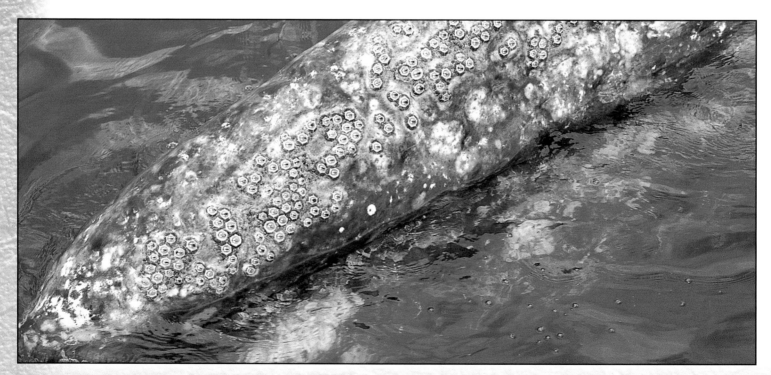

Large host creatures like this whale take no notice of their tiny barnacle passengers.

LIVING TOGETHER

A useful partnership between two different animals is called a symbiotic relationship. Usually one half of the partnership provides protection in exchange for food or cleaning services from the other. Animals that would otherwise be aggressive learn to recognise their helpful partners and do not harm them.

The remora fixes itself to sharks with a sucker on its head. It feeds on parasites on the shark's skin. Remoras have even been found clinging to the roofs of sharks' mouths.

Tick-birds feed on parasites found on the skin of large mammals. Both animals benefit from this – the bird gets fed, and its host, here a giraffe, is kept clean.

Amazing FACT

Despite its very slow speed, the sloth is a popular host. The sloth moth spends its entire adult life living in the fur of a sloth, apart from briefly hopping off to lay its eggs in the sloth's dung. And it is not alone – one sloth was found with more than 950 beetles living in its fur!

Moth on a sloth's fur.

Animals of all sorts travel long distances every year to find the best places for feeding or breeding, but birds make some of the most incredible journeys of all.

INCREDIBLE JOURNEYS

Young swallows form a group to find their way to South Africa. Young cuckoos make a similar journey, but they do it alone. The tiny ruby-throated hummingbird flies 1000 kilometres over the Gulf of Mexico without a break. Bar-headed geese fly over the Himalayas, at altitudes where humans can barely breathe.

Migrating birds often fly in a V-formation. The lead bird 'breaks up' the air, making flying easier for the birds behind it. Leading the pack is tiring, so birds take it in turns.

Amazing FACT

The Arctic tern holds the record for long-distance migration. Every year it flies from the Arctic, where it breeds, to Antarctica, where it spends the winter – and back again. The round trip can be 40,000 kilometres, often over open sea where there are no landmarks to help it navigate.

Arctic tern in Scotland.

HEADING SOUTH

In summer, many birds build their nests and lay their eggs in Europe and North America, where food is plentiful. Then, when the weather begins to turn colder, they set off on the long journey to Africa or South America, where they can spend the winter in the sunshine. In spring they fly north again. Changes in the weather and in the length of the days trigger their departure.

Not all migrations are long-distance – every summer the blue grouse makes a short trip downhill to lay its eggs.

After a journey of thousands of kilometres, swallows often return to exactly the same spot to build nests.

NAVIGATING

Exactly how birds navigate, or find their way, is a mystery that puzzles scientists. Landmarks like coastlines and rivers play a part, but many birds migrate over open oceans. The positions of the Sun and the stars probably help birds in clear weather. In cloudy conditions birds may use the Earth's magnetic field to help them find their way.

At night the stars indicate which way is north.

During the day the Sun moves from east to west.

27

It is not just birds that migrate. Many other animals, from massive whales to fragile butterflies, also make extraordinary journeys.

Grey whales give birth in the sea off Mexico, then travel 16,000 kilometres to the food-rich Arctic seas.

OCEAN WANDERERS

Whales, turtles, eels, tuna fish and salmon all migrate thousands of kilometres. Green turtles swim 2000 kilometres to lay their eggs. Salmon return from the sea to the rivers to breed, swimming 2500 kilometres upstream. They leap up waterfalls as they go.

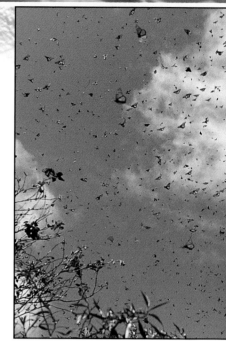

Monarch butterflies swarm 3000 kilometres south to Mexico from North America.

When storms bring cooler water, spiny lobsters travel south. They march along the seabed in single file.

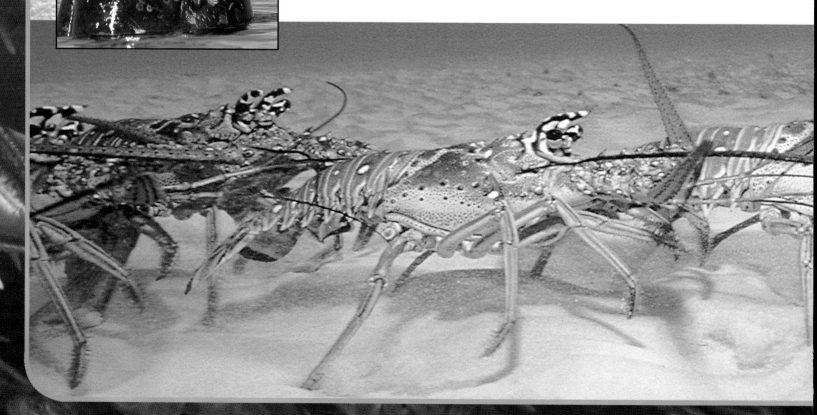

INSECTS ON THE MOVE

Monarch butterflies are famous for their epic migrations, but many butterflies and moths travel several hundred kilometres in search of food and nest sites. Plagues of desert locusts can travel in a swarm of 40 billion, covering an area of 1000 square kilometres and requiring 80,000 tonnes of food each day.

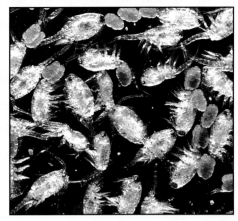

Shrimp larvae.

Amazing FACT

The minute members of the shrimp family that are plankton migrate on a daily basis. They can sometimes travel as far as 500 metres in a day, as they swim to the surface to feed on smaller plant and animal plankton.

Just 7 centimetres long, baby eels swim 5000 kilometres from the Sargasso Sea to Europe.

Running

• Coyotes are fast sprinters, reaching speeds of 65 kilometres per hour to catch jackrabbits.
• Even the bulky rhinoceros can charge at 45 kilometres per hour and can turn quickly.

Climbing

• The chamois can climb 1000 metres in 15 minutes.
• Common toads have been found at heights of over 8000 metres.

Gliding

• The Bismarck flying fox, a type of bat from New Guinea, can have a wingspan of 1.65 metres.

Hopping

• An unfed flea can jump 600 times an hour for 72 hours without stopping.
• Hares can hop at speeds of up to 56 kilometres per hour.

Flying

• A hummingbird in a zoo hovered non-stop for four hours, in which time it must have beat its wings more than one million times.
• American woodcocks fly no faster than human walking speed!

Swimming

• Brotulid fish have been found at depths of more than 8000 metres.
• Seahorses have a top speed of 0.016 kilometres per hour.

Slithering

• The deadly black mamba from Eastern Africa can slither along at 19 kilometres per hour.

Journeys

• After leaving the nest, sooty terns spend 3–4 years of their life in the air without landing.
• European painted lady butterflies travel over the Mediterranean Sea.

GLOSSARY

adapted
Having skills or features which help an animal, plant or person to survive in a particular place.

aerodynamic
Shaped to offer the least resistance to air.

buoyancy
The ability to float in liquid.

contract
To become shorter.

elastic
Material that returns to its original shape after being stretched.

flexibility
The ability to bend easily.

invertebrate
An animal without a backbone, such as a worm or jellyfish.

mammal
A warm-blooded animal that gives birth to live young.

navigate
To find one's way from one place to another.

plankton
Tiny animals or plants that float along with the water current.

polyp
A small sea animal that combines with others to form colonies.

predator
An animal that hunts and eats other animals, called prey.

simultaneous
At the same time.

stability
The ability to keep one's balance.

streamlined
A pared-down shape that cuts smoothly through water and air.

vertebrate
An animal with a backbone, such as a snake or an elephant.

31